AF507183

Copyright © 2022

ISBN: 9798352064450

Creepy Crawly Counting

By Taylor Thorne

1 ONE cicada killer is flying by alone.
"Come and follow me, I'll show you to my home.
I burrow in the ground instead of living in a hive.
I lay lots of eggs and take cicadas down alive.
I feed them to my babies so they can grow like me!
(By the way, I am a wasp, though I look like a large bee).
I know how to sting but I wouldn't want to.
Stay away from me and I'll stay away from you!"

2 TWO saddlebacks, spiny caterpillars,
say, "Look but don't touch! Our venom is a killer.
But only if you eat us, we warn with colors bright.
We are still just babies and we don't want to fight.
We're vegetarians, eating leaves all afternoon.
We have to eat a lot for when we go in our cocoon.
When we emerge, we're much less neon green.
We'll be brown moths. Fluttering is our dream!"

3 THREE wheel bugs say, "Hello! We know we look scary.

Spiky wheels upon our backs, if you see us please be wary.

We have a giant fang – it's how we stab our prey.

We try not to bite humans, but if you pick us up we may.

We come from a big family. They call us the assassins.

Just when bugs think they're safe – BAM! That's when it happens.

This is how we prep a meal. It's just Mother Nature.

Just like you, we need to eat, plus we keep your garden safer!"

4 FOUR dragonflies ask, "Can you hear us buzz?
We zoom around the pond! We're so excited 'cause
we spent years underwater – two years in the muck –
but now we have our wings. We symbolize good luck!
Did you see us dip our tails? That's how we lay our eggs.
We eat mosquitos from the air. We catch them with our legs.
We see almost everything. We have the biggest eyes.
Uh-oh, look out! Here comes a bat!
Come on, we gotta fly!"

5 FIVE garden spiders say, "We know we look massive.
We can be deadly predators, but to humans we are passive.
Even if we were to bite, our venom would not harm you.
We just want to spin our webs which other bugs get stuck to.
We will keep your gardens free and clear of any pest.
Aphids, flies, mosquitos, wasps are snacks we can digest.
But that's not all we eat – we make a dangerous date.
If we're feeling peckish, we'll make dinner of our mate!"

6 SIX roly-polys say, "You'll meet our cousins next.
We know a special trick to keep predators perplexed.
We hide our squishy bellies, we give ourselves a hug.
We look like tiny spheres – it's why we're called "pill bug!"
'Exoskeleton' is what we call our back.
It's made of many hard plates, an armor against attack.
We're not any type of insect – we're technically crustaceans.
Shrimp and crabs and barnacles are a few of our relations."

7 SEVEN millipedes shout, "We're the prettiest for sure!
These are just a few of us, but there are many more.
Our name speaks for itself, just look down at our feet.
We have lots and lots of legs. The way they move is neat!
We are decomposers, which means we eat the dead stuff.
We help to clean the forest floor. Fall leaves are quite delicious.
We come out in the nighttime or when it's cool and wet.
Sometime, lift a rock or log, you'll find us there, I bet!"

8 EIGHT aphids drinking sap say, "Come, let us show you
our super special mouthparts for extracting sticky goo!
Because we slurp so much of this, when we go number two
you'll see a sugary substance – we call this honeydew!
This attracts the fungi, which seals this poor plants fate.
We'll move on to the next one and start to congregate.
We really are a nuisance to farmers everywhere.
Our families are gigantic and we sip more than our share."

9

NINE fireflies (depending who you ask,
some call them lightning bugs) say, "We have the task
of lighting up backyards with special rhythmic blinking
to find someone to love, a little bit like winking.
We are toxic beetles, though we may look gourmet.
Bioluminescence keeps predators at bay.
Our numbers are declining, we need a darker night.
If you want to see more of us you must produce less light!"

10 TEN mayflies swarming sob, "We are all that's left
of our horde of thousands, it makes us feel bereft.
Not sure how we're talking, we don't have any mouths.
We only live a day or two and die fast as we've roused.
But our kind lived with dinosaurs, we're terribly resilient.
We have not evolved much, our designs already brilliant!
You can tell a stream is clean if you find us there.
Fish will eat us if they jump and snatch us from the air."